The Red Squirrel Book

by Jane Russ

GRAFFEG

Dedication

For MT.
...am still here 'squirrelling'.

Contents

5   Introduction

9   The Red Squirrel

23   Red and Grey Squirrels

39   ...and the Pine Marten

45   Habitat

53   Activity

63   Feeding

77   Breeding

85   Threats, Predators and Diseases

91   Mid Wales Red Squirrel Partnership

99   A Squirrel's Tale

103   The Red Squirrel in the British Consciousness

110   Photo credits

112   Acknowledgements

Introduction

It is 1962 in Crownhill, Plymouth, Devon and there is a jumble sale underway. My ten-year-old self has just spent 3d (half of my weekly pocket money) on an old book, *How I Tamed the Wild Squirrels* by Eleanor Tyrrell with illustrations by Honor C. Appleton. It marks the moment when I fell in love with this mischievous, agile and engagingly charming animal. I would have been lucky in the sixties to actually see a red squirrel, although there were still small pockets of population in Devon.

It is 1997 and we are staying in a bothy on an estate in Scotland. It is about 6am and I am asleep, when suddenly there is urgent knocking on the bedroom door. 'Quick, quick, there's one on the front lawn.' Our friend didn't have to say what 'one' was, we had all been waiting to

How I Tamed the Wild Squirrels
by Eleanor Tyrrell

catch a glimpse of a 'red' and at last I would experience the intense excitement of seeing one in the wild.

The red squirrel is firmly embedded in the consciousness of the British Isles.

Any wild animal in its natural habitat is a thrill but this small, inquisitive creature with its characteristic bouncing 'run and pause' gait and breathtaking climbing ability can hijack your enthusiasm. Although it has only a tiny amount of myth and legend to speak of and, once you have excluded the few items just a slim selection of art and literature, the red squirrel is firmly embedded in the consciousness of the British Isles. I hope, by the end of this book, you too will be captivated and that it will be a lasting love affair with one of Britain's iconic mammals.

The Red Squirrel

The scientific name for the red squirrel is *Sciurus vulgaris* and it has an interesting, charming derivation. *Sciurus* (the sub-genera used for eight different species of tree squirrel) is an amalgamation of two Greek words, *skia* which means 'shadow' and *oura* which means 'tail'. The translation would therefore be 'the animal who sits in the shadow of its tail'. Not quite so delightfully, *vulgaris* just means 'common'.

Squirrels are rodents; they belong to the order *Rodentia* from the Latin *rodere* 'to gnaw' and of the sub-order *Sciuromorpha* (squirrel-like). Within the *Sciuromorpha*, red and grey squirrels both belong to the family *Sciuridae*, genus *Sciurus* and species *vulgaris* for red and *carolinensis* for grey. In the past the classification for red squirrels was based on coat colour which can be very confusing with many different colour 'morphs' to be found. Modern developments in molecular biology using DNA and mitochondrial DNA are creating queries about previously held beliefs concerning the validity of some sub-species. The complete *Rodentia* order may well be revised over the next few years in the light of these developments. Research continues in this area.

The defining feature of rodents is that their teeth wear and are regrown throughout their lives, this is true of both red and grey squirrels. In fact reds and greys are similar in most things. The comparative skull photographs opposite show the similarity as well as the difference in profile. Generally however, one could say that they both have a flat scull, large eyes and small ears (although the red has some long ear tufts in

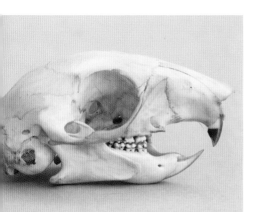

Grey Squirrel *Sciurus carolinensis*
Overall length 58.9mm, overall width 33.6mm.

Red Squirrel *Sciurus vulgaris*
Overall length 50.6mm, overall width 30.9mm.

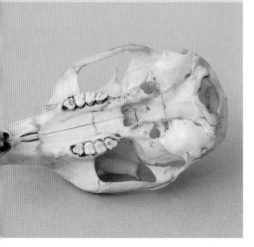

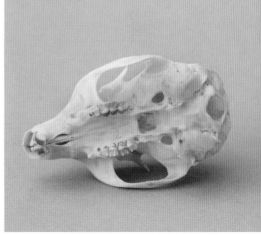

winter). The average body length is also not markedly different, with the red having a length of 22cms to 26cms in the grey, not including the tail. It is in weight, however, where they differ most. The red has a weight average of 300g, whilst the grey is a heftier 550g, which may explain the grey's stockier, more solid overall look when compared to the lithe red. There will be slight variations in weight according to season and male to female too.

The silhouette for both squirrels is long in movement and tight and short when sitting, with the characteristic 'question mark' outline. The front legs are short 'arms' which act as shock absorbers on landing. The front paws have four sharp-clawed toes and a vestigial, tiny thumb, all of which are used to deftly manipulate nuts, pine cones and other food. Interestingly it has been shown that squirrels can be right- or left-handed

"... an animal who needs to come down trees as fast as it goes up, double-jointed back feet."

when they eat a pine cone. The long powerful back legs are used for leaps of up to six metres and have five toes and, double jointed feet, very useful for an animal that needs to come down trees as fast as it goes up. The very strong claws on both feet give the squirrel the ability to hang, up or down, totally flat to a tree trunk or branch.

The long tail is useful for balance and support but also for 'talking' between animals in both colours. The chattering cross grey squirrel in your back garden will be using his tail to cuss and swear at your cat and then later to signal 'who are you' to another grey squirrel. The tail can also offer shade in the summer and be curled snuggly around the body in the drey to keep warm in the winter.

Perhaps rather surprisingly, the colour of red squirrels varies considerably between individuals, from season to season, from location to location, and also by age. Reds moult their body-fur twice a year, in spring and autumn. The tail-fur and ear-tufts moult only once, in the autumn, with, as you would expect, a bushier tail and thicker coat being the norm in the winter. The spring moult goes from head to back legs and the autumn moult from tail to head.

The summer and winter colour differences are very marked. Research in Europe suggests that there may be a correlation between darker squirrels surviving for longer in dense, dark evergreen forests and brighter reds being helped by

By the time the body moults in late spring or early summer the tail may be completely creamy white.

the camouflage of dappled sunlight (particularly if you included their white venter or underbelly) in broad-leafed woodland.

A rich chestnut colour is most likely in the summer, with a white stomach. There may even be some grey fur around the head and sides. The coat is a coarser, shorter length on the body than in the winter and the tail can become rather straggly and thin, like the ear tufts, which may be completely missing during the months from June to September.

The autumn moult can occur at any point from August to November, the replacement winter coat being longer, thicker and a richer, darker colour, with white underparts as in the summer. This is the point when the annual tail moult takes

place; it too becomes thicker, with denser hairs, and the ear tufts return looking long and luxurious.

From its onset, the winter coat also slowly bleaches, getting gradually paler beginning from the tip of the tail, that by the time the body moults in the late spring or early summer the tail may be completely creamy-white. Confusingly, not all red squirrels have a cream tail or even a cream tip, and the body colour can be anything from russet red to dark brown and even in some cases, black (melanistic). I think it's safe to say that it is hard to generalise about the coat of red squirrels; every squirrel is an individual.

Red and Grey Squirrels

Red and grey squirrels

Fossil remains have been found of an ancient squirrel; it is hard to pinpoint exactly how old but one can say that there were squirrels on the British Isles between 7,000 and 10,000 years ago. They arrived and colonized just before this island broke away from the continent of Europe; they were the last mammals to do so. They were also to colonize Ireland before it broke away from England, Scotland and Wales.

It would seem from bestiary notes in the margins of manuscripts and carvings in churches, that squirrels were certainly noted in the medieval period. The density, of course, is not known as nobody kept records. It was said in the thirteenth century that forests in Ireland were so dense that a squirrel could travel from one side of the country to the other without putting a foot on the ground. However, with the spread of agriculture, deforestation gradually thinned the numbers and by the end of the fifteenth century, they were extinct on the island of Ireland. The current Irish population of red squirrels was re-introduced into the country between 1819 and 1856.

Squirrels have such a stronghold in Scotland that it will seem unlikely to us now, they were all but extinct there by the beginning of the eighteenth century. This was due to the decimation of habitats through the need for timber for building, fuel and of course that ever present de-nuder of forests – war. Habitat clearance was, and always will be, an issue for the red squirrel. The cycles of woodland growth can be seen to move with the rise and fall of animal numbers, nationwide. Felling that leaves copses of trees

isolated is bad news for squirrels in general and reds in particular. The tree canopy is the motorway of the squirrel world and connectivity is key. Between 1772 and 1872 red squirrels were re-introduced to Scotland (as they had been to Ireland) and the planting of new conifers helped their establishment.

From 1860 onward, squirrel numbers rose nationally, peaking in 1890 when the woodlands planted across the country became mature enough to sustain a burgeoning population. During this period gamekeepers helped numbers grow by keeping down predators to protect the game birds, who coincidentally predated on squirrels. Soon damage to woodland was noted by owners and the pendulum swung the other way. 'Squirrel clubs' soon became a fashion, and it became socially acceptable to hunt and shoot them.

At the turn of the nineteenth century red numbers were possibly higher than in the previous several hundred years. However, from 1900 onwards there was a gradual but serious drop in the red population and, owing to the introduction of the grey squirrel at over thirty sites between 1876 and 1929, the red has never really recovered. By the 1930s it was common enough to see reds but they never again gained the abundance of previous years. Greys spread into areas where red numbers were declining to fill the 'squirrel void' and, since the 1940s, the spread has been relentless. This means that in the majority of the south of England the red is extinct, with only small pockets of population remaining. The last red was seen in London in

Grey squirrels can withstand the ravages of squirrel parapoxvirus.

1942 in Regent's Park.

We know from previous experience that red numbers ebb and flow but, with the introduction of the grey, suddenly there was another animal to move in and fill the gap before numbers had a chance to recover. The decline in red numbers from the 1900s onwards seems, on scrutiny of the figures, not necessarily to be influenced by the arrival of the greys. Greys were not present in every area where red numbers declined and the declines continued, with or without greys. What greys did, however, was prevent the recovery of the reds following a red decline.

Did greys 'kill off the reds'? There are as many reports of co-existence as killings. Hybridization is not an issue. We have already discussed the variety of colours in the red and this may have led to people thinking that there had been interbreeding. However, it would seem that these sightings were just that: wrongly attributed greys.

More importantly, grey squirrels can withstand the ravages of squirrel parapoxvirus (SQPV) which they brought with them from North America when they were introduced into this country. It may not kill them but they are carriers and it can easily be imagined how quickly it can spread through a red population in any given area. Mortality in reds seems to be 100% after contact with SQPV. In 2003, computer modelling of the decline of reds, allowing only for the straight introduction of greys, does not actually mirror the speed of the decline, but add in the effects of SQPV and the decline fits far more closely. It is worth noting that the

decline in Scotland and Ireland is markedly lower than England and Wales. This could be because SQPV is not present in these greys as, when brought in, they came from a different source to those introduced into England. There is no easy answer to the decline of this iconic mammal but it would certainly seem that SQPV has played its part.

Physique also has played it's part. The grey, as already discussed, is larger and heavier than the red, thus giving it the capacity to store more fat for winter survival. There are also more grey kittens born per litter and they live in higher densities than the reds.

Furthermore, habitat is a clue to the successful takeover by the greys. Broadly speaking, reds live in areas of mainly mature conifers and greys live in areas of mature broad-leaved trees. For building dreys and food, reds favour Scots pine, larches, or Norway spruce. Their food sources will be small seeds and cones which are not high enough nutritionally for greys. Greys favour oak, beech, hazel and sweet chestnut; they can digest acorns which reds cannot unless fully ripe and, in general, take in much larger quantities of food than the red. However, greys are happy to live in areas containing both conifers and broad-leaved species and perhaps this adaptability is the key to their takeover. Reds need larger numbers of conifers to reach high densities, whilst greys can go for both. Reds will live in mixed woodland (particularly on islands) but it is in the competition for food where the greys always win. Not only will they rush to dominate the food

There are pockets of red squirrel resistance against decline in Scotland, the Isle of Wight, Brownsea Island and Anglesey.

supply of what is available and in quantity right now, but they will steal cached food saved by reds for later in the year. This has an effect on young reds particularly as they can find it hard to build up enough fat to cover them for survival in a bad winter and to become next year's breeders. It can be seen, therefore, that a population of reds will decline and eventually become extinct. Woodland containing mainly conifers but with occasional broad-leaved trees would be a good habitat for greys but reds would be under threat if there are greys present. When numbers are high they will, of course, move into each other's territory. Long-term fluctuations in numbers is dependant on habitat; short-term fluctuations on food supplies i.e. pine cones and

acorns respectively. (It has to be said too, that greys have adapted to the urban nature of modern day life, visiting gardens and parks and feeding on whatever they can find; reds will do this to a lesser extent but only in safe red areas.)

In the last several decades we have become aware of the importance of our native species. There are pockets of red squirrel resistance against decline in Scotland, the Isle of Wight, Brownsea Island and Anglesey. Let us hope that the combined efforts of conservation partnerships, like the Mid Wales Red Squirrel Partnership described later in this book, together with legal measures and local government, will lead to the slow reintroduction of the red squirrel throughout the British landscape.

...and the Pine Marten

Amazingly, it would appear that the pine marten, a natural predator of the squirrel, may be helping to raise red squirrel numbers. Like the reds, pine martens were once very common in Britain. However, the loss of habitats so beloved of the reds and a drive by Victorian gamekeepers to keep them from the pens of bred shooting-birds, meant numbers dropped dramatically. Eventually, pine martens were to be found only in remote areas of Scotland.

A study in March 2018 proved unequivocally what had been believed anecdotally for some time; that the re-introduction and recovery in the numbers of pine martens runs parallel to a marked increase in the number of red squirrels in the Borders, central region and Highlands of Scotland. When pine marten numbers rise, grey squirrel numbers fall: it would seem that greys in their original habitats in North America, have no natural predator of the pine marten-type and are therefore not sufficiently wary of them.

Like squirrels, martens are arboreal and the lighter red has the ability to escape the marten's clutches on slimmer branches than its heavier grey counterpart. Furthermore, the grey is more inclined to spend time on the ground, where it is easy pickings for the fast and agile pine marten.

The 2018 research concerns the balanced relationship between the three mammals. Evidence was gathered using sticky patch traps to collect hair samples from feeders containing their favourite foods. The samples were subsequently tested

for DNA. Ireland had been the first area used to look at this relationship but this Scottish research has made it official: the more pine martens, the fewer greys, the more reds. Although it may take decades to re-establish the red squirrel in areas lost to it at present, this is a really clear indication that it is feasible and that the pine marten may be the key.

Habitat

The ideal balanced red squirrel habitat would have a mixture of deciduous broadleaved and coniferous trees. The most important thing is that the trees are seed producing. Reds can cope in an environment on either side of this mix, just broadleaved or just coniferous, although in the later scenario it needs to be principally mature trees of 20+ years to ensure a steady supply of food.

Reds never live in the kind of densities that greys do. Greys will populate from four to ten times more heavily than a comparative red population (typically one or two reds per hectare to five or six greys per hectare). This sheer volume of grey bodies in any given area means that, as young reds grow up, they cannot compete for food, are measurably under weight and few survive their first year. This is important because if a red kitten can survive its first year then it has a good chance of making it to three or four. The reds will continue to breed but the numbers do not appreciably increase and so, as the mature population dies off, they are not replaced fast enough and will eventually become extinct in that location.

Reds, except during the breeding season, are solitary and not really territorial. They will have a 'home range' but will not usually defend it against other squirrels. The exception to this rather relaxed attitude are females, who will defend their home range against other females during the breeding season and stay close to the nursery drey once the kittens are born. It is hard to tie down a specific area required by a red as it will change

with the season, the density of other squirrels, and the abundance of food. Finding a mate can make for an expansion in a male range, whilst suckling mothers may close down their range somewhat while the kittens are young.

The density and abundance of the forest canopy, combined with low berry-producing shrubs below and thick ground vegetation to aid fungus production, may make for a smaller range in one year, whilst a larger range may be needed the following year if the seeds fail in any one species of tree, or if there is a very wet spring when even fungus will not thrive. Some trees, such as beech, only produce seeds in quantity every four or five years, so variety in the habitat can be very important. A tree producing a poor crop in one year may have a bumper one in the next.

The arboreal red lives in the tree tops, using the branches to move around the forest. It is possible they

spend anything up to 70% of their time in this canopy without needing to come to ground. This simple fact makes it clear that, as forests are 'rationalized' for profit, smaller isolated large copses might only see a red passing through, moving on to a better habitat elsewhere. Of course a forest is the first choice for the squirrel but it is highly adaptable and can survive in suburbia provided there are sufficient parks/wooded gardens/hedges where it can find food growing and that can be used as a red squirrel super-highway. *In extremis* it can also resort to the bird feeders now so popular in town gardens. Imagine looking at the connectivity of the landscape – would a squirrel survive where you live?

Activity

Walk into a woodland area where you know they are present, stand still and be prepared to be patient.

Although not nocturnal, red squirrels can be very hard to see, being arboreal mammals and living most of their lives in the trees. They have a simple but effective hiding technique; if you keep walking through their woodland they just circle the tree they are climbing, ensuring they are permanently out of sight. The best tip for catching sight of one is to walk into a woodland area where you know they are present, stand still and be prepared to be patient.

In spite of much disinformation to the contrary, squirrels do not hibernate. They do, however, have a shorter period of daily activity during the winter months when the days are shorter and colder. This may be as brief as only four hours after dawn, peaking in the middle of the day. During exceptionally bad weather they may miss a day actively feeding, but any prolonged break from the daily routine can cause severe loss of condition. Several days of intense, persistent cold without feeding can result in death. There is a temperature balancing act to be considered for the poor squirrel. Like many small warm-blooded mammals, it has to balance not only energy to find food, but maintaining core temperature throughout. In the colder months this is crucial. Squirrels in general store little body fat, red squirrels in particular. The question therefore is: is it better to stay in a warm drey for slightly longer or risk going out to find food that may or may not be there and use any energy one has left to keep warm once back at the nest?

Being diurnal, the single daily peak of activity in the middle of a winter's day will gradually change as daylight hours lengthen, to two peaks during the spring with a rest about midday when the temperature is at its highest. In the longest daylight months of the summer, activity will begin just before sunrise and will consist of two longer periods with a proper 'siesta' around noon, the afternoon activity not being quite as busy as the morning session. It has been suggested that the afternoon rest in the drey or tree nest helps with digestion when food is plentiful.

The weather affects activity as you might expect; frost, mist and fog reduce it, whilst strong sunshine increases it. Interestingly, it would seem humidity plays its part too, with animals more active on dry days than damp ones, but that seems logical if one is wearing a fur coat!

Feeding

What red squirrels eat, and when, depends on the season and the type of woodland.

Squirrels are herbivores, although the term granivore describes them more accurately as they are eaters of seeds as opposed to grazing mammals. In fact they are not exclusively herbivores as they will take bird eggs, some chicks, and have even been known to catch full-grown birds up to blackbird size if the opportunity presents itself. What they eat, and when, very much depends on the season and the type of woodland. This table assumes a squirrel in a perfect mixed broad-leaf and deciduous woodland.

Spring	Summer	Autumn	Winter
tree flowers	conifer seeds	pine, hornbeam,	pine seeds, buds
fruit blossom	conifer shoots	hazel, beech, oak	and needles
elm seeds	fruits	and walnut seeds	fungi
conifer flowers	insects	fruit, bramble,	insects
pine seeds	birds eggs	damson and apple	roots
pine buds	fungi	fungi	
pine shoots	green leaves	insects	
bark tissue	roots		

One may be surprised to see fungi on the list, not a food stuff generally associated with squirrels. However, it is a very important secondary food and is often taken from the ground to dry off in the tree canopy wedged in a tree fork. Fungus *Vuilleminia mycelium* found under the bark of dead or dying oak trees is a food source in the winter, as is the sappy tissue stripped from trees as the sap rises in the spring.

In pine forests, the cones are eaten first as shoots; later, in the summer, as green cones and finally, the reds will continue to feed on the full cone until the following spring when the last remaining seeds drop. Cones are meticulously stripped of each individual scale, leaving the stump to be discarded in a telltale pile of scatterings on the forest floor. It can be easily understood that reds in a pine forest can spend most of their time in the canopy, whilst greys living amongst broad-leafed trees will spend much more time on the ground.

In deciduous woodland greys have an advantage if there are many oaks present as they can digest the tannins found in acorns more easily than the reds. However, hazelnuts are a great favourite with both squirrels as are sweet chestnuts. Squirrels find food by smell and they are well known for sniffing at the spiky shell of a sweet chestnut

only to discard it untouched. On inspection, these discarded shells usually have small or undeveloped nuts inside, the weight of the shell acting as sign of a good nut as well as the scent.

Naturally, the type of food and the proximity of it to the drey are also important. It is easy to understand that the energy required to actually find and remove seeds from pine cones is considerably more than that needed to eat just one or two large sweet chestnuts found close by. This energy versus quantity is another constant balancing act. It would appear that in a pine forest, half the time spent away from the drey is spent in foraging for and eating food.

During the autumn when, hopefully, there is an abundance of food, the squirrel will start caching food for

winter. This may mean that the animal is so focused and busy that it will stop for short rests out of the nest between foraging sorties. Here the crucial issue is for the squirrel to eat enough to keep going but hide enough to secure its winter supplies.

During caching, a hole is dug, maybe two centimetres deep, the seed/nut is put in and covered quickly with both forepaws. There may be more than one squirrel working at this task in the same area and it is not uncommon to see another squirrel dig up the just buried nut and cache it somewhere else for themselves. (It has been recorded that some squirrels do a fake burial, not actually adding the nut but covering it as thought they have to put off marauders.) Of course not all seeds/nuts hidden in this way are ever recovered by the animal that hid them, many will just go on to germinate and become saplings. I have personal experience of this with grey squirrels in our garden in Banbury in Oxfordshire. Over a period of just under ten years, they buried and forgot about so many beech nuts in our garden from the tree next door that the saplings (which I dug up and potted on) were sufficient eventually to make up a large section of the hedge at the side of my daughter's garden.

Naturally, trace minerals will be eaten in very small quantities in ingested soil, and calcium too, in the form of bone or antlers, is obtained when the squirrel sharpens its teeth. Captive squirrels are usually offered bones to gnaw on for this reason. Water is not a problem as the moistness of the food and dew supply what is needed but squirrels will drink from streams and standing ponds in a dry summer.

Breeding

There are no rigid and absolute fixed timings for squirrel breeding as it is very dependent on weather conditions, food supplies, and the age and condition of the female. A rough rule of thumb would have the first mating of the year somewhere between the beginning of December and the end of February but good weather conditions could bring it forward and bad ones delay

it. Later in the year during the spring/summer mating period, if a seed crop fails, breeding may be abandoned all together. There are two peaks for births, mid-February to mid-March and June to July.

The male squirrel has an inactive sexual period from approximately September to end November. During this period the testes will retract into the body cavity and the scrotum will be empty. Gradually they will descend again as the breeding season gets closer and be fully functioning to coincide with oestrous in the female. Females are polyoestrous, with potentially two periods of fertility in a good year; however, this period only lasts one day. In the lead up to this day the female's scent is obviously changing; she marks her 'home' area and males overlapping it will start to show an interest. This will culminate on the day itself in a fast and furious mating chase with the female and usually several males, rushing through the canopy, spiralling up and down the tree trunks; with the fastest finally mating with the female. Young males may nip in and mate with her too, and these 'satellite males' are sometimes favoured by the female, who will ensure they get a chance. The study of genetics has moved on so much in recent years that genetic fingerprinting is now able to prove conclusively that litter mates may in fact have been fathered by different males.

Like hares, squirrels are solitary animals and do not live in male and female pairs. They have what is called a 'promiscuous' mating cycle, meaning that any male can mate with any female; having done

so the male takes no further part in the rearing of the young. Gestation takes approximately five to six weeks during which time the female will build or re-work an old drey into the nursery drey. From the outside a drey looks a somewhat ramshackle affair made of twigs and leaves, almost round and nestling in the fork of a tree trunk, usually about six metres or more from the ground. (These are much easier to see in deciduous woodland in the autumn when the leaves have fallen.) In the summer there may be more than one drey in use at any time and these summer ones are more of a resting and cooling-off spot than a permanent home. They will usually be in use until they collapse. The winter drey, however, is of a much more solid, snugger construction, still rather 'loose' looking from the outside, with a thick woven casing, often made from twigs of the host tree, but warmly lined with moss, leaves, grasses, wool and fur, and situated in a more protected site to withstand the ravages of winter wind and rain. The pregnant female may use an already constructed drey to have her kittens, just lining it with extra moss and fur, or build a new one from scratch often slightly removed from her other dreys; this usually takes about two to three days.

Once the young are born, the mother will not venture far from the drey and its hairless, toothless, blind, deaf and helpless occupants. They only weigh 10 to 15g and she is very aggressively protective of them for the first two months. The female is equipped with four pairs of nipples which are very difficult to see before the kittens are born, but once they are suckling they become progressively easier to see as a bald circle is worn around each one. Litters can be as few as one or as many as six offspring, with three the average. Summer litters tend to be larger than spring ones and these kittens will have the advantage of

They will start to take solids by about week seven with weaning occurring at any point from eight to twelve weeks, and it is about this time that the kittens will begin to explore outside the drey.

being older before they have to face a winter alone. At between two and three weeks the hair starts to cover the whole body, and by five weeks it has gained density so that the kittens are starting to look like miniature squirrels. The eyes and ears should be open by five weeks and the teeth, which will have been budding since the second week, will all be through by about week six.

They will start to take solids by about week seven with weaning occurring at any point from eight to twelve weeks, and it is about this time that the kittens will begin to explore outside the drey. Milk teeth will be complete by ten weeks and the young squirrels should be fully weaned and have moulted into their first seasonal coat by sixteen weeks. How much maternal support the youngsters get will depend on whether another litter is to be raised that year, which as we have seen, is itself dependent on food supplies and the weather. If a second litter is likely, the juveniles will be out as independent young animals, developing their own small 'home ranges' close to the litter drey. It has been recorded that sometimes the female may tolerate the young born in the summer to stay close during the autumn and winter, but by the spring mating they will definitely be on their own. The milk teeth will be shed between four and eight months but not the incisors; these

will continue growing throughout the squirrel's life and be ground down by wear.

Interestingly, the recognisable squirrel behaviours of the red are not learnt from the mother but are inborn. Drey building, posture, and caching are all inherent techniques, however, these do appear to get better with practice as do the agile and exhilarating skills of climbing and jumping.

If the juvenile squirrel can weather its first winter, then it is likely to survive for at least another year. However, 75 to 80 percent of youngsters will die in their first one. Starvation, poor weather conditions, and disease are almost certainly the most important mortality factors, as are road traffic accidents.

Threats, Predators and Diseases

The slash felling of an isolated large copse can wipe out a small population as they literally have nowhere to go.

Squirrels, both red and grey, are hosts internally and externally to many parasites; the external ones – fleas, ticks, mites and lice – don't really seem to bother them. A squirrel kitten will inherit its mother's fleas in the nursery drey: *Monopsyluss sciurorum* and *Taropsylla octodecimdentata* (Eastern Scotland) are to be found on the red, *Orchopeaus howrdii* on the grey, all are occasionally seen on the other type. Internal parasites include ringworm and roundworm, with perhaps the most serious problem being a type of enteritis coccidiosis caused by the parasite *Eimeria sciurorum*. This not only affects the gut and therefore general condition but, if an infected squirrel is put under stress conditions, it can lead to death. As already discussed in chapter three, for the red squirrel, the most challenging disease of all is squirrelpox virus or SQPV.

Predators are relatively few for the red. The pine marten, as mentioned earlier, whilst taking some, has easier pickings from the ranks of the greys and is even helping red numbers to rise. Wildcats, polecats and stoats, if present, can form a threat as can foxes and domestic dogs and cats who will take a squirrel on the ground if they can catch it. Finally, birds of prey will take a squirrel, larger birds taking bigger, older animals, with smaller falcons and hawks taking younger juveniles. Whilst there is some predation, in general it does not seem to be a serious worry for the survival of the red squirrel.

Bearing in mind the speed and height that they move through woodland, it might be expected that some squirrels would be lost to what could be called 'natural accidents', falling, drowning, burning; however, by far the biggest natural loss will be to starvation. We have seen in past chapters what a knife edge the squirrel balances on to maintain its condition, and a bad seed crop, combined with poor weather and perhaps a weight of parasite infestation, will soon cut through a population.

Man of course plays his part in squirrel deaths, not as a hunter now that reds are protected, but the destruction of habitats can have a

marked influence on their survival. The slash felling of an isolated large copse can wipe out a small population as they literally have nowhere to go. Road traffic accidents too account for some deaths and rope bridge crossings have been built in some areas across busy roads to help with this. In the larger scheme of things, long-term climate change will definitely have an impact on the sustainability of conifers, one of the prime habitats for red squirrels in the north of the UK. The connectivity of habitats has been mentioned already and the fragmentation in the planting of new forests will cause problems in the future. Conservationists and landowners need to play the long game, to ensure that not only the red squirrel but other endangered species of birds and mammals are considered when replanting.

Mid Wales Red Squirrel Partnership

Mid Wales Red Squirrel Partnership

The Mid Wales Red Squirrel Partnership (MWRSP) was established in 2002 and The Partnership aims to expand and protect the unique population of red squirrels in mid Wales; one of only three significant red squirrel populations in the whole of Wales.

The MWRS Partnership is working to gather a sound baseline of information about the red squirrel population in mid Wales; leading to the development of a robust understanding of the work required to conserve the red squirrel in mid Wales.

Conservation efforts include:

• Establishing a buffer area around red squirrel strongholds with control of grey squirrels

• Ongoing monitoring of the red squirrel populations

• Advising landowners and forest managers on habitat improvements to benefit red squirrels

• Using forest planning to maximize the value of forests to red squirrels

The grey squirrel has been identified as one of the main threats to the survival of the red squirrel, a threat which can only be mitigated with sustained local action.

Partners
To this end they are working with partners, all of whom can help in some aspects of the conservation efforts. The main partner is The Wildlife Trust of South & West Wales.

The Wildlife Trust
South and West Wales
De a Gorllewin Cymru

Other partners are: Carmarthenshire, Ceredigion and Powys County Councils, Natural Resources Wales, The National Trust, Tilhill, Selectfor and other private forestry companies and interested individuals.

The number of red squirrels that still remain in mid Wales is difficult

Above: *MWRSP member and Forester Huw Denman (left) giving a tour of his woodland to a group from the Welsh Government agri-environmental scheme Glastir. The visit was designed to show how suitable habitat management combined with grey squirrel control can create the right conditions for red squirrels.*

Above: *MWRSP Volunteer Rhian Mai Hubbart (left) with Graduate Ecologist, Becky Blackman from Carmarthenshire County Council (right) installing a series of camera traps at Clywedog forest near to Llanfair Clydogau.*

to estimate; they are elusive and numbers can fluctuate dramatically from year to year. However, local ecologists estimate that between 100 and 500 red squirrels are present in the forests surrounding Llyn Brianne reservoir which encompasses parts of Powys, Ceredigion and Carmarthenshire. The large conifer plantations that are strewn across the hills of mid Wales are very poor habitat for any squirrel. Ironically, it is this very fact that has made the Tywi Forest and surrounding plantations a sanctuary for the red squirrel. The lack of available food for squirrels in conifer plantations means that these woodlands offer the greatest potential for supporting red squirrels in the presence of grey squirrel expansion, as small-seeded conifers are less favoured by grey squirrels.

However, even-aged plantations dominated by Sitka spruce only support low densities of red squirrels and slight alterations in woodland management in these areas can significantly improve the habitat for red squirrels, while still disadvantaging the greys. A diversity of tree species is important to reduce the impact of poor cone years in one particular species; species of value to red squirrels include Norway spruce and lodgepole pine. To retain connectivity, forest areas need to be designated for long-term retention, preferably at the edges of plantations where coning is heavier. Retaining links between seed-producing areas will help to prevent the isolation of red squirrels from each other, from food sources and will help to reduce losses from predation.

MWRSP is working with forest managers in the mid Wales red squirrel focal site to try to ensure that the conifer woodlands, that are so vital to the survival of the red squirrel in mid Wales, are managed not only for timber, but also with red squirrels in mind.

Local communities too have their part to play by helping to control grey squirrels in the towns and villages surrounding the focal area. Volunteers also play a major role in undertaking forest surveys for red squirrels. Becky Hulme, Red Squirrel Officer for the WTSWW explains. "There are many people in the local communities of the mid Wales red squirrel focal area, who are keen to see the red squirrel thrive once again

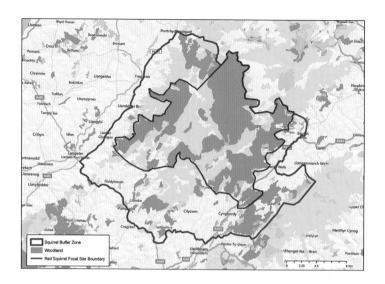

in mid Wales. If we all work together, we are hopeful that the red squirrel will once more become a common sight in our woodlands and gardens."

The MWRSP website has a reporting facility which enables users to access maps of previous sightings and record their own sightings of red squirrels helping to build a picture of activity in the focal area. The website is designed to encourage greater awareness of the plight of the red squirrel in mid Wales and to inspire even more people to get involved with their conservation.

midwalesredsquirrels.org

Above: *Boundary map for the Mid Wales Red Squirrel Focal Site and buffer area.*

A Squirrel's Tale

This is the wonderful story of Decan Andersen who saved a squirrel kitten that fell from the fourth floor guttering of his apartment block into his garden. The tiny squirrel was only 10cms long, about four to five weeks' old, and badly injured with a gash in its chest.

To begin with Decan did not want to take the squirrel in, he thought the mother would come and sort it out. She did come, looked the small body over and then left it, probably deciding there was nothing to be done. Decan couldn't bear the thought of it being left to the elements so he took the baby squirrel in and immediately sought advice from the local vet and Wildlife Preservation group. Whilst waiting for them to call back, he put the tiny body beside his female cat Coco, who stepped up at once and cleaned the baby and cuddled up to it to keep it warm.

The wound was dressed by the vet and Decan took on the mammoth task of cleaning it every three hours, and bottle feeding the baby squirrel (found to be male and now called Tintin) kitten milk every four. It was hard to keep the bandages on the tiny chest so Decan had to get creative. This was when he came up with the idea of making tiny t-shirts out of old socks to keep the cut clean and scratch proof. With all this help it still took nearly five months to heal and for Decan to be able to stop using the t-shirts.

Of course, after so much human and cat contact, the young squirrel was now in a state where he had no fear of predators. After long consultations with the Danish Wildlife Preservation group and the vet, everyone agreed that Tintin would find it hard to survive in the wild. Decan's next job was to build a cage, well, less of a cage more of a castle. The door is never closed of course and Tintin is free in the house and a full member of the family. He only uses the cage to eat in, and to use his toilet tray.

Decan bought him a ferret harness; although it would be wonderful if Tintin could roam free outside, in fact he really feels very insecure and won't leave the house without it on. There are lots of natural predators in the woods and gardens close by the flat, including cats, hawks and owls (dead birds and squirrels are not unusual). Tintin understands that the harness keeps him safe and that the lead will take him straight back to Decan if he gets frightened.

If you are interested in meeting Tintin and Decan and reading about their daily routine, do have a look at Tintin's website at www.tintinthesquirrel.com where there are some lovely films of what life is like with a squirrel.

Having read this book about the somewhat driven life of wild squirrels, you can probably appreciate how hard it is to have one in your home. Decan absolutely does **not** advocate keeping squirrels as pets and, as red squirrels are an endangered species in many countries, he has been given special dispensation by Danish Wildlife Preservation to keep Tintin to the end of his natural life.

THE TALE OF SQUIRREL NUTKIN

BY

BEATRIX POTTER

F. WARNE & CO.

The Red Squirrel in the British Consciousness

'...and then, as it has virtually no real myth and legend or art and literature to speak of, there will be a short chapter on The Red Squirrel in the British Consciousness'. On hearing this so many people said, 'Oh but you will mention The Tufty Club? Tufty was such a part of my childhood.'

The Tufty Club
Tufty (full name Tufty Fluffytail) started life as a character in a series of books by Elsie Mills in 1953. The Royal Society for the Prevention of Accidents (ROSPA) was looking for a way to raise awareness of road safety in children under five. Tufty featured in a number of leaflets on road safety for ROSPA and eventually in 1961. The Tufty Club was born.

The following year it was expanded to include older children, a nationwide network of local groups was established and more than 60,000 children had been enrolled. There were monthly meetings and 'road shows' with games, reading of the books and all including a road safety message. The number of club branches varies depending on whose figures you believe, but everyone agrees that by 1972 over two million children had become members.

Perhaps as memorable as the badge were the information films on television. Life was slower, gentler then; Tufty always called his mother Mummy and held her hand. Willy Weasel was the naughty child who didn't go with his Mummy to the ice cream van, ran out into the road and was knocked down and lost his ice cream on the tarmac. There were never gory scenes of Willy flattened by a car; he just lost his treat. The general message was put very clearly, and definitely had an effect on lowering the road accident figures involving children.

Tufty continued to spread his message throughout the '80s and continues to be a residual presence for ROSPA. He had two re-workings of his look in 1979 and 1993 and is still used in print and in packs for schools. Today, road safety for children involves the speed of the car and survival rates at that speed. Possibly the idea of teaching children to be active participants in road safety might be a better way to tackle the problem.

The Tale of Squirrel Nutkin
The only other important squirrel figure in British consciousness was created by Beatrix Potter in her book *The Tale of Squirrel Nutkin*.

First published in 1903, Potter sets her story in the middle of a lake. Whilst staying in the Lake District in 1901 she started drawing and writing *Nutkin*; Derwentwater and St. Hubert's Island can clearly be seen in her illustrations.

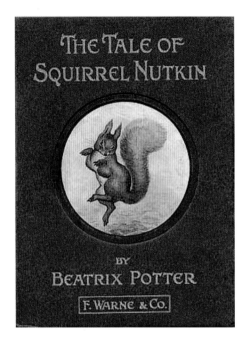

Every day, Nutkin and his squirrel chums bring Old Brown, the owl who presides over the island, offerings to secure the rights to collecting nuts there. They cross the water each morning with their little sacks and return in the evening. (Regarding the offerings, interestingly, although we see a picture of the squirrels fishing and the idea of them collecting beetles seems possible, there is

does not respond and gradually the squirrel gets braver and braver, until finally he jumps on the owl's head:

'Then all at once there was a flutterment and a scufflement and a loud "Squeak!"'

The other squirrels scuttered away into the bushes.

When they came back very cautiously, peeping round the tree—there was Old Brown sitting on his door-step, quite still, with his eyes closed, as if nothing had happened. But Nutkin was in his waistcoat pocket!'

When Nutkin reappears to join his friends, having been taken inside his house, we see that Old Brown has got his own back by removing half of Nutkin's tail.

It is an exposition about the link between actions and consequences.

never any explanation of how they catch the mice and the mole that are two of the earlier owl gifts in the story!)

This is the tale of a tail. On each of the six consecutive days the squirrels visit, they bring Old Brown his gift and each day the naughty Nutkin goads the owl with a riddle. (Riddles were popular at the time and here, the riddles are left for the reader to interpret.) The owl, however,

Squirrel Nutkin in *The Tales of Beatrix Potter*, the ballet.

In 1971, Squirrel Nutkin appeared in the film of a ballet choreographed by Sir Frederick Ashton called *Tales of Beatrix Potter*. (Nutkin was danced by Wayne Sleep.) Just over twenty years' later, Anthony Dowell reworked it slightly and it was seen on stage at Covent Garden for the first time, with Matthew Hart as Nutkin. In the original film, the masks and costumes were groundbreaking and in his stage production Dowell also worked with the mask-maker Rostislav Doboujinsky and designer Christine Edzard.

The music was a reworking of melodies taken from Offenbach, Sullivan and others by the composer John Lanchbery, with new original sections linking them together. Lanchbery conducted for the 1992 Covent Garden production too.

The costumes and particularly the masks were hard for the dancers, who had only a restricted view through specially created eye holes which were then gauze covered. Doboujinsky used cycling helmets as the base form for some of them. It must have been very disorientating spinning or jumping when you couldn't really see where you were going. The effect, however, was wondrous and, although rather too long and not universally approved of by the critics, audiences loved it. Subsequently, there have been revivals in 2007 and 2010.

Right: Steve McRae as Nutkin in the 2007 production.

Photo credits by chapter

Front cover: © Andy Wilson
Back cover: From left to right:
© Maggie Bruce, © Kevin Sawford
© Claire Cameron: www.flickr.com/
clairecameronphotography; www.facebook.
com/clairecameronphotography, © Robin
Morrison

Introduction
Page 4: © Andy Wilson
Page 5: © Jane Russ
Pages 6-7: © Franz Komlosi

The Red Squirrel
Page 8, 18, 20-21: © Kevin Pigney
Page 11: © Will Higgs: www.skullsite.co.uk
Page 12: © Andy Wilson
Page 13: © Claire Cameron
Page 14: © Catriona Komlosi
Page 16: © Beverley Thain
Page 19: © Andy Wilson

Red and Grey Squirrels
Page 22 btm left and top right:
© Natasha Weyers
Page 22 btm right, 29, 31: © Claire Cameron
Page 22 top left, 25, 26, 28, 32, 35:
© Andy Wilson
Page 36: © Catriona Komlosi
Page 37: © Maggie Bruce

...and the Pine Marten
Page 38, 43: © Kevin Pigney
Pages 40-41: © Claire Cameron
Page 42: © Ellis Lawrence

Habitat
Page 44: © Andy Wilson
Page 47, 48-49: © Kevin Sawford
Page 50: © Maggie Bruce
Page 51: © Catriona Komlosi

Activity
Page 52: © Claire Cameron
Page 55: © Kevin Sawford
Page 56: © Catriona Komlosi
Page 57, 58-59: © Andy Wilson
Pages 60-61: © Robin Morrison

Feeding
Page 62, 66, 67, 72-73: © Catriona Komlosi
Page 65: © Kevin Sawford
Page 69: © Kevin Pigney
Page 70: © Robin Morrison
Page 75: © Claire Cameron

Breeding
Page 76: © Catriona Komlosi
Page 78: © Hedera Baltica
Page 79: © Willamette Biology
Page 81: © Gilles Gonthier
Page 83: © Peter Trimming

Threats, Predators and Diseases
Page 84: © Kevin Pigney
Page 87, 88-89: © Catriona Komlosi

Mid Wales Red Squirrel Partnership
Page 90: © Andy Wilson
Page 93, 94, 96: © Becky Hulme: Mid Wales
Red Squirrel Partnership
Page 97: © David Wilcock

A Squirrel's Tale
Page 98, 100: © Decan Andersen

**The Red Squirrel in the British
Consciousness**
Page 103, 106, 107: © Beatrix Potter
Page 104: © Jane Russ
Page 109: © Alastair Muir

Acknowledgements
Page 113: © Maggie Bruce

Every effort has been made to trace
copyright holders of material and
acknowledge permission for this publication.
The publisher apologises for any errors
or omissions to rights holders and would
be grateful for notification of credits and
corrections that should be included in
future reprints or editions of this book.

Acknowledgements

It has been a joy to select the pictures for this book and my first acknowledgement has to go to the marvellous photographers, whose generosity make this such a delight to read. I know I always say I could not do it without you but it is true. I could not do it without you! Thank you so much, I never take your support for granted.

Gilly Middleburgh came up trumps as the first line of proofing on this volume and deserves many thanks. To all my chums that continue to cheer me on from the sidelines. It never gets any easier to draw out the words but your continued encouragement drives me on. Thank you.

Finally, for some serious pictorial support concerning how to draw a squirrel for the endpapers; thanks to my grandson Arlo Jenkins (aged 5).

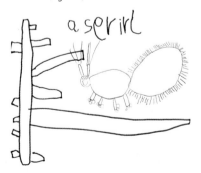

a serirl

The Red Squirrel Book
Published in Great Britain in 2018 by
Graffeg Limited

Written by Jane Russ copyright © 2018.
Designed and produced by Graffeg
Limited copyright © 2018

Graffeg Limited, 24 Stradey Park
Business Centre, Mwrwg Road,
Llangennech, Llanelli, Carmarthenshire
SA14 8YP Wales UK Tel 01554 824000
www.graffeg.com

Jane Russ is hereby identified as the
author of this work in accordance with
section 77 of the Copyrights, Designs
and Patents Act 1988.

A CIP Catalogue record for this book is
available from the British Library.

ISBN 9781912654178

1 2 3 4 5 6 7 8 9

Squirrel photography can be hard,
photobombing even happens here.

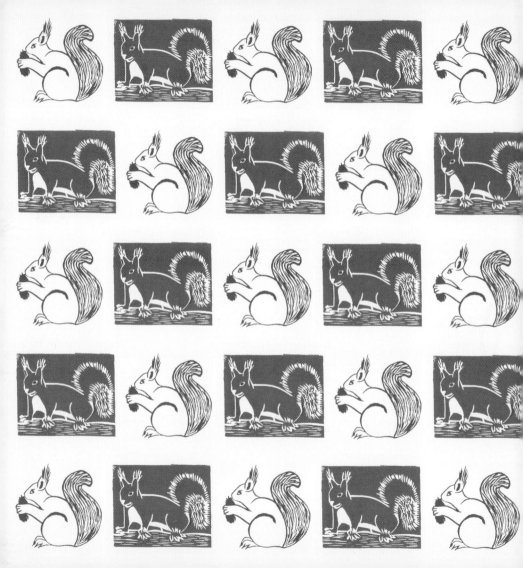